AF575659

GROUND

K5 Railgun

Krupp's WWII Behemoth

DAVID DOYLE

Library of Congress Control Number: 2022944451

Designed by Justin Watkinson
Type set in Impact/Minion Pro/Univers LT Std

ISBN: 978-0-7643-6644-4
Printed in India

Published by Schiffer Publishing, Ltd.
4880 Lower Valley Road
Atglen, PA 19310
Phone: (610) 593-1777; Fax: (610) 593-2002
Email: Info@schifferbooks.com
Web: www.schifferbooks.com

Acknowledgments

This book would never have seen the light of day without the generous assistance of the following individuals and organizations: Pierre-Olivier Buan, Thomas Anderson, Tom Kailbourn, Greg Heuer, Jim Gilmore, Scott Taylor, and the staff of the Ordnance Museum. In particular, the Lord has blessed me with a wonderful and supportive wife, Denise, who accompanied and helped on the many research expeditions required to put this volume together.

A work crew stands by as a 20.3 cm Kanone Eisenbahnlafette is rolled, rear end first, up slightly inclined tracks onto a firing platform, termed a Schiessbettung in German. This firing platform, or firing bed, visible to the far right, pivoted at its center, allowing the entire railroad gun and carriage to be traversed 360 degrees. *Bundesarchiv*

CHAPTER 1

The K5(E) in Combat

With the rise of Hitler, Germany initiated several programs to produce railroad guns in the 1930s. In addition to the authorized long- and short-term development efforts, Krupp initiated its own design program. The result of the Krupp program would be the rail gun produced in the greatest quantities and the subject of this volume: the 28 cm Kanone 5 Eisenbahngeschütz (railroad gun). The name is often abbreviated to 28 cm K5(E).

The K5 gun barrel was originally designed with twelve deep grooves. A full-size barrel was proof-fired at Krupp's test range in 1937, and the following year a complete K5(E) was undergoing tests. This was the 28 cm K5(E) Ausf. A, which incorporated a Sprengwerk, or supporting structure for the barrel. Series production began with the Ausf. B in 1937, two examples of which were built. These guns also featured the Sprengwerk but had an improved traversing mechanism—the K5(E) had a very limited traverse of 2 degrees for fine target alignment. The Ausf. C followed, and by 1940 eight guns of various Ausführung were in service. Some of the early weapons suffered from barrel splits, leading Krupp to redesign the barrel, with the depth of the grooves being reduced to 7 mm. This barrel is sometimes referred to as the K5 Tiefzug 7 mm. While this greatly reduced the problem, cracking was not completely eliminated until the Vielzug barrel was introduced in 1943.

Twenty-four examples of the K5(E) were built by Krupp and Hanomag, two of which (919443 and 919447, although 919214 was later converted to 31 cm glatt configuration as well and, in fact, was captured by US forces and shipped to the US in glatt configuration) were experimental 31 cm smoothbore weapons. The weapons were deployed as two-gun batteries. A battery consisted of five officers, fifty-six NCOs, and 169 enlisted men. Each gun had a forty-two-man crew, twenty-five of whom were actually involved in operating the gun. The battery was deployed in three sections (Zuge), with each section moving as its own train. The 1.Zug included thirty-four railcars, including special ammunition boxcars, passenger cars, and railcars to transport kitchen equipment and food, and, although towed by a steam locomotive for long distances, a diesel locomotive was included in the train. When the train reached its destination, the steam locomotive was dispatched for further service elsewhere, and the diesel locomotive, with its notably reduced exhaust plume, stayed with the weapon. It was used for shunting the gun and cars as needed, its lesser exhaust aiding concealment.

The 2.Zug and 3.Zug each included a gun and about twenty cars. The gun trains included, of course, the K5(E), specialized cars for the K5 ammunition, a flatcar for transporting the generator (which would be placed on the K5 upon emplacement), more antiaircraft guns, a temperature-controlled car for use with the ammunition, flatcars for transporting the turntable sections, and a crane to put those pieces in place, as well as a mobile repair shop.

Two primary variations of the K5(E) were manufactured: the Ausf. C and the Ausf. D. While the total number of guns is known, the exact number of each of these Ausführung that were produced has not yet been determined. From the ground, the most-notable difference between the Ausf. C and Ausf. D is the different style of aiming stations used on the two designs.

The guns were initially deployed along the English Channel to support the aborted invasion of Britain (Unternehmen Seelöwe, Operation Sea Lion). Four two-gun batteries—710, 712, 713, and 765—were deployed in the areas of Calais and Boulogne. From their position, the English coast was inside the 64,000-meter range of the K5(E). Subsequently, the weapons were used during the invasion of the Soviet Union, participating in the sieges of Sevastopol', Leningrad, and Stalingrad, before returning to the

Mistakenly identified in a British War Office report as a 28 cm Bruno Neue (New Bruno), or "28 cm Br N K (E)," a mistake repeated by later writers, including earlier works by this author, this is in fact a Krupp prototype for the K5(E) 28 cm railroad gun and is believed to be the sole example of the 28 cm Kanone 5 Eisenbahn Ausfrung A, or 28 cm K5(E) Ausf. A. The massive gun is shown in the Krupp plant. The large supports along the base of the barrel are Sprengwerk, reinforcements for the barrel, believed to be required due to its great length and weight. In fact, this reinforcement was proven to be unnecessary, and after the first three weapons its installation was discontinued. *Thomas Anderson collection*

French coast, where in 1944 they became part of the famed Atlantic Wall defense. Battery 688 fired on Gold and Juno Beaches and the surrounding area before shifting its targets to the Caen area in August. That same month, Battery 765, stationed near Malaunay, fired at Allied forces near Rouen. In Lorraine, Battery 640 fired on the US XX Corps and engaged in a duel with US artillery firing 240 mm howitzers and 8-inch guns, with one of Battery 640's guns being heavily damaged and subsequently withdrawn for repair.

Eisenbahnbatterie 712 was to be dispatched to North Africa, but due to German losses there, instead the K5s saw action in Italy, most notably at Anzio. While there, the two guns of Battery 712 fired 523 rounds at Allied forces, causing a severe shortage of 28 cm ammunition across all the batteries. Eisenbahnbatterie 686 was withdrawn from the Eastern Front in mid-1944, in large part due to the lack of ammunition. In September 1944 the remaining batteries in France—688, 710, and 713—were redeployed to the Netherlands.

In December 1944, during the Battle of the Bulge, the Germans fired 388 28 cm rounds from K5(E) and ninety 31 cm rounds from K5 Glatt at Allied forces.

This press photo, released in late April 1940, is believed to include the first four production K5(E) railway guns, with their massive 28 cm barrels elevated. Each barrel had a removable liner with rifling. The first K5 liner had twelve grooves 10 mm deep, but after some of these liners developed splits after firing, they were redesigned with grooves 7 mm deep, and this solved the problem. A good view is also provided of the gun's cradle. *Thomas Anderson collection*

The same four K5(E)s are deployed in line, their crews evidently performing drills. These would represent the railroad guns of two railroad batteries, or *Eisenbahnbatterien*, each battery being assigned two K5(E)s. In early 1941 there were four *Eisenbahnbatterien:* nos. 710, 712, 713, and 765, stationed in France on the English Channel coast. Later, other batteries and detachments would be assigned K5(E)s, and the batteries would see service on the Eastern Front in the sieges of Leningrad, Sevastopol', and Stalingrad, only to return to France to defend against possible Allied landings along the English Channel.

Although a two-gun railroad battery comprised an impressively large complement of personnel and equipment, the dense railroad networks of Europe enabled the Germans to dispatch these potent weapons, such as these two batteries, nearly anywhere they were needed. *Thomas Anderson collection*

Part of the crew of a K5(E) poses next to the weapon as it rests on the firing bed of a turntable in 1941. Total personnel of a K5(E) train comprised forty-two men, with twenty-five men and two electricians serving the gun systems. There were six officers and noncoms as well as three electricians to operate the generator, temperature car, and other systems.

Crewmen are preparing a K5(E) for operations on a Vögele turntable. Canvas tarps were draped over the gun during transit, both to protect it from the elements and to camouflage it. Toward the right, several crewmen are maneuvering the ammunition crane into place to lift ammunition from the truck up to the roof of the generator housing.

Ammunition for a 28 cm gun is stacked on the bed of a truck at a K5(E) battery site in France in July 1940. Although railroad flatcars were generally used to transport ammunition from the ammunition cars to the railroad gun, sometimes trucks also performed the work of shuttling projectiles, powder bags, and cartridges to the gun.

In France in 1941, crewmen hoist 28 cm ammunition from a flatcar to the deck on the roof of the generator housing of a K5(E). One ammunition round for the 28 cm gun comprised the projectile (*Granate*), several propellant bags, and a metal cartridge case with a propellant charge. The metal cartridge was the last element to be placed in the breech. *Bundesarchiv*

Once the ammunition had been hoisted to the generator housing's top deck, crewmen placed the ammunition on a trolley and rolled it forward on tracks on the deck to the breech of the 28 cm gun. The propellant bags (*Vorkartuschen*) are light colored. The projectile is at the bottom center of the pile, and the metal cartridge case is to the left. *Bundesarchiv*

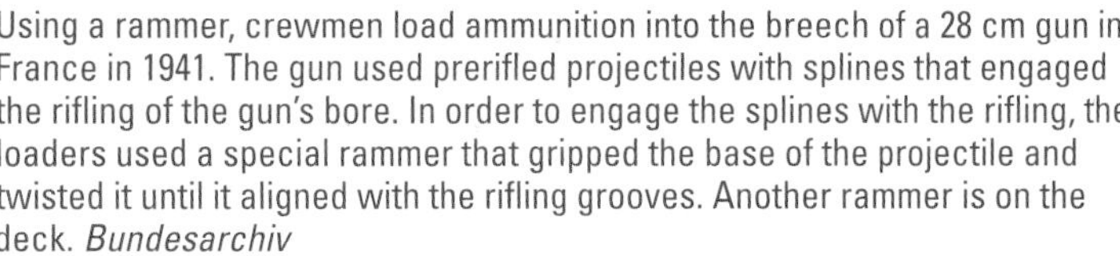

Using a rammer, crewmen load ammunition into the breech of a 28 cm gun in France in 1941. The gun used prerifled projectiles with splines that engaged the rifling of the gun's bore. In order to engage the splines with the rifling, the loaders used a special rammer that gripped the base of the projectile and twisted it until it aligned with the rifling grooves. Another rammer is on the deck. *Bundesarchiv*

A crewman operates the breech of a K5(E) in France in June 1941. The breechblock was of a horizontally sliding design. In 1943, Krupp experimented with an interrupted-screw breech for this gun, with the intention of eliminating the metal cartridge in favor of bagged charges, but plans to deploy this type of breech were discontinued. *Bundesarchiv*

A photographer captured this view from above the breech of a K5(E) railroad gun facing aft, somewhere on the Eastern Front on June 22, 1941, the day the Germans invaded the USSR. The two men behind the breech appear to be cleaning the barrel. Behind the man at the rear is the ammunition crane. Following the K5(E) are other railroad cars.

A K5(E) is positioned on a Vögele turntable, with a flatcar to the right. On the side of the car body, a crewman is standing at the gun-control station, also called the aiming stand. This station featured a detachable platform, steps, folding top cover, instrument panel, and controls for traversing the carriage and elevating the 28 cm gun.

The crew of a K5(E) stands at order, prepared to serve the gun. Behind the two loaders, immediately to the rear of the gun's breech, is a fully laden ammunition trolley, aft of which are other loaders. Two operators stand next to the ammunition crane. To the far left are two men sighting the piece at the gun-control station. Two crewmen, presumably electricians, stand at the ready on a platform alongside the generator housing. To the far right is a tripod for a gun-laying or calibrating optical device.

The 28 cm gun of a K5(E) on a Vögele turntable is elevated for firing. Near each end of the firing bed of the turntable was an electric motor that drove the inner two of four rollers (the rear outer right roller is visible here), thus powering the traverse of the gun. There were also provisions for traversing the firing bed by means of hand cranks geared to the two inner rollers. Just above the top center of the car body is the sleeve and cradle that supported the barrel and was mounted on the trunnions. *Thomas Anderson collection*

A gunner on the side of the generator housing pulls (or pretends to pull) the firing lanyard of a 28 cm gun positioned on tracks. Maximum elevation of the piece was approximately 50 degrees. Minor traversing adjustments of about 1 degree to either side of center were possible by shifting the carriage's position with reference to the front truck. *Bundesarchiv*

Two crewmen work at the gun-control station of a K5(E) in France, sometime in 1941. The gunner to the right is operating the controls. In front of his waist is a large handwheel that regulated the speed of the gun's elevation and the mount's traverse. Above that wheel was mounted a sight. Two cables support the cover over the control station. *Bundesarchiv*

The gunner of a K5(E) 28 cm rail gun is at his controls, on the left side of the gondola. He is peeping through the sight and is grasping the handwheel that controlled the speed of elevation and traverse of the gun. He is standing on a platform made of steel grille, and above him is a hinged cover in the raised position.

In this view of a K5(E) on a turntable in France in July 1941, nearly the entire firing bed is visible. Faintly visible to the far right is the turntable recoil mechanism. Hidden within the carriage, the elevation mechanism was linked to the bottom of the diagonal arms of the cradle, through the sleeve of which the gun barrel passed.

In a hilly locale, a K5(E) is situated in a prepared emplacement. The ammunition crane is visible toward the right. In the left foreground is a railroad flatcar, beyond which is visible the front truck. Although the 28 cm gun is at or near full elevation, it probably was not engaged in firing, since no crewmen are to be seen on or around the piece.

A K5(E) on a curved section of track appears to be prepared for firing in Armsheim, Germany, in March 1940. The king post of the ammunition crane extends down below the crane platform and is inserted in a bearing on a beam running across the rear of the generator housing. Protruding from the rear frame of the truck are two buffers.

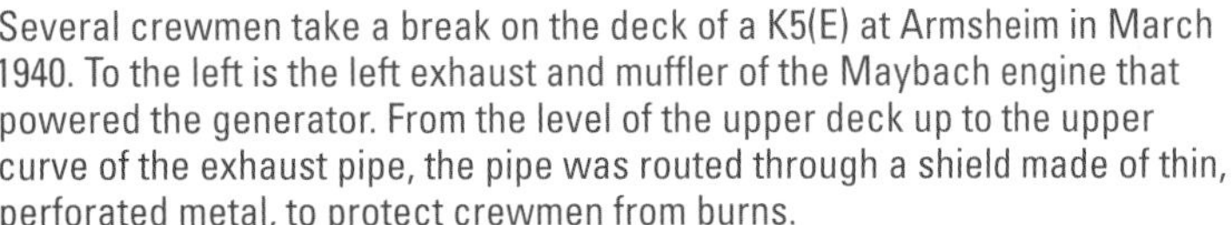

Several crewmen take a break on the deck of a K5(E) at Armsheim in March 1940. To the left is the left exhaust and muffler of the Maybach engine that powered the generator. From the level of the upper deck up to the upper curve of the exhaust pipe, the pipe was routed through a shield made of thin, perforated metal, to protect crewmen from burns.

Crewmen collect along a K5(E), the barrel of which is at high elevation. In the background is a ladder. The ribbing cast into the barrel sleeve to give it additional strength is visible. To the rear of the gun's breech is a deck panel with wooden slats running across it. Called the *Ladeklappe*, this was raised after the gun was loaded, before firing.

When practicable, *Dombunker*, or cathedral bunkers, were built near K5(E) firing positions, in order to protect these valuable assets from bombing when not in use. Here, a K5(E) of Railroad Battery 713 is being moved out of a bunker near Hydrequent, France, in 1941. The bunker, which had armored doors, was constructed of concrete with earth banked against it. *Bundesarchiv*

A K5(E) departs from a cathedral bunker in France in 1941. Cathedral bunkers were long enough to house the two railroad guns of a battery and a locomotive. In 1940, three railroad-gun bunker sites were established between Calais and Boulogne, France: at Calais, Pointe aux Oies, and Hydrequent. Later, another one was built at Coquelles. *Bundesarchiv*

In the Alban Hills in Italy in March 1944, K5(E) "Robert" sits outside a railroad tunnel in which it was concealed between firing missions against the Allied beachheads at Anzio and Nettuno. Two K5(E)s named "Leopold" and "Robert" were used in this sector. Crewmen are engaged in the frequent task of cleaning the bore of the gun. *Bundesarchiv*

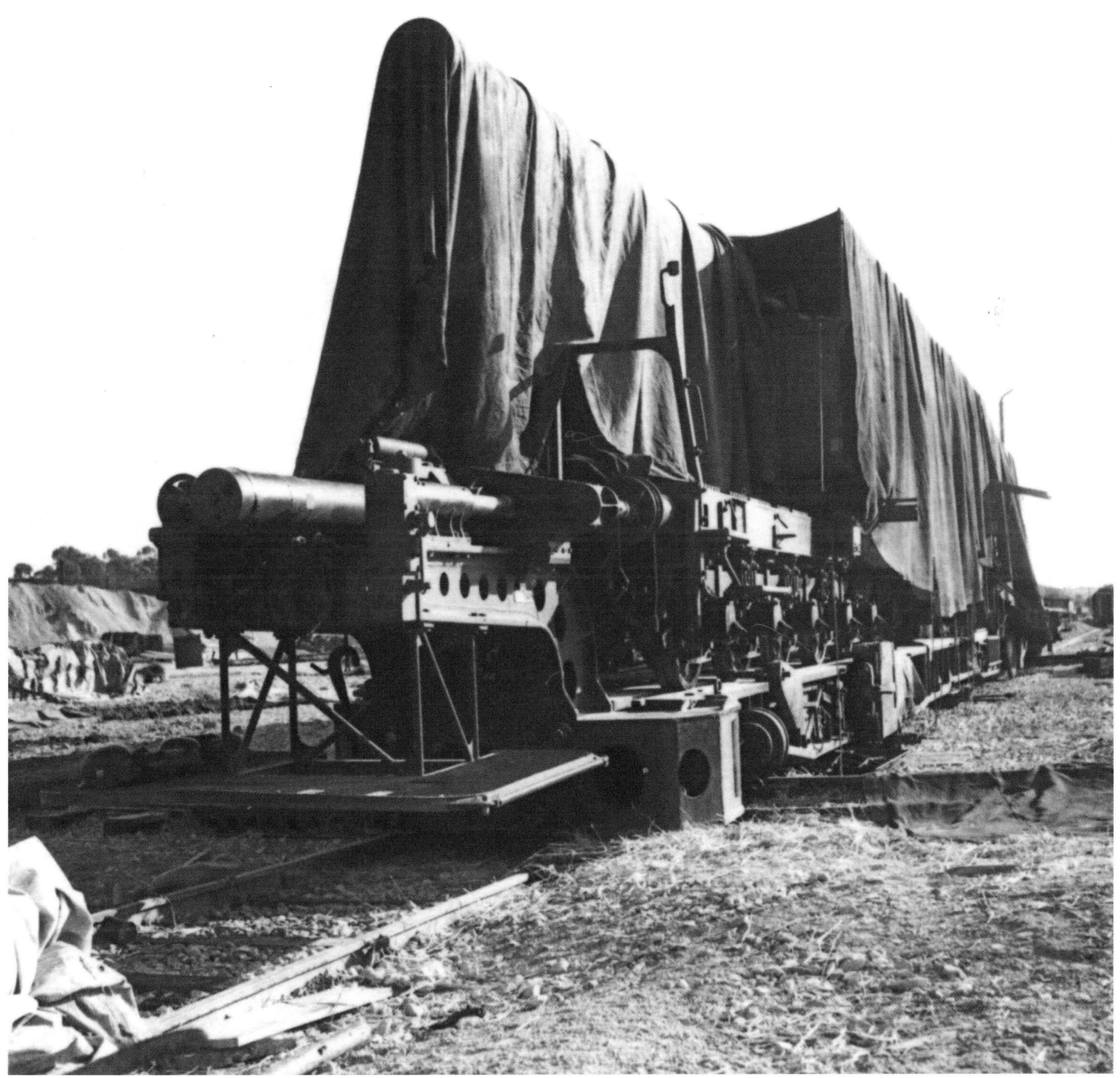

This mysterious-looking hulk is a K5(E) under tarps, viewed from the front left as it rests on a Vögele turntable somewhere in France in August 1940. In the foreground is the turntable's recoil mechanism, which traveled around the turntable track in unison with the front of the railroad gun and buffered some of the gun's recoil when fired.

At a firing site in 1940, a K5(E) sits on a Vögele turntable, partially covered with tarps. Visible to the front of the forward truck is the curved side of the recoil mechanism, perforated with large lightening holes. Aft of the rearmost tarp, the ammunition crane and the left exhaust pipe of the Maybach generator engine can be seen.

Thirteen crewmen of a K5(E) pose in relaxed style on a supply flatcar behind their railroad gun in Armsheim, Germany, in March 1940. Behind them is the ammunition crane on top of the generator housing, partially covered with a tarpaulin. On each side of the crane is a handwheel for operating the crane. Also visible are the guardrails of the crane.

Some of the crewmen are at their stations on this K5(E) in Armsheim, Germany, in March 1940. Two gunners are at the gun-control station toward the left. On the platform toward the right are two men, probably electricians, attending to the generator. The men on the firing deck appear to be cleaning the barrel. They are holding a rammer staff.

At a French site in 1941, a K5(E) and its train have been moved out of a bunker. Behind the railroad gun is a flatcar, followed by several boxcars of different types. These boxcars would have included ammunition cars and a temperature car. Usually the compact WR360C14 diesel locomotive was used to shunt the trains at firing bases. *Bundesarchiv*

Three railroad guns, including a K5(E) to the left, were photographed in a yard. Crewmen check over various sections of the gun, visit with neighboring crews, or go about their business in the yard. The two railroad guns at the center and right appear to be captured French models, of which the Germans pressed numerous examples into service.

The same K5(E) railroad gun seen in the preceding photo was photographed from an angle farther to the front. The purpose of the cage-shaped structure above the front truck is unknown; it may have been a framework for a canvas cover. The wheels visible below the car body, or gondola, belong to another railroad vehicle in the distance.

This K5(E) was photographed in or near Sevastopol, Crimea, at the time of the 1942 siege of that city. The generator housing is the separate structure to the rear of the gondola. The gun tube is secured with a cable to its travel lock, on the top front of the gondola.

Photographed in or around Sevastopol at the time of the 1942 siege, this K5(E) appears to be the same one in the preceding photo, probably at the same location. To the right is one of the numerous types of railroad cars that were required in the operations of the K5(E) batteries, including ones for transporting crewmen and support personnel, ammunition, food and field kitchen, antiaircraft artillery, field workshop, temperature-control apparatus for the ammunition, auxiliary generator, and the turntable and firing bed and related equipment.

A K5(E) paused on a railroad track somewhere on the Eastern Front has guardrails erected along the sides of the top of the gondola. The platform and cover for the gunner's station are deployed on the side of the gondola.

A K5(E) has taken up a firing position on a turntable at an unidentified location. The right rail of the firing bed is visible below the trucks. The firing bed was a straight pair of tracks on which the K5(E) rested when being deployed on a Vögele turntable. In the foreground is a tripod for a sighting device. Dangling from the crane to the left is a sling for hoisting ammunition trolleys. An ammunition trolley is on the top of the generator housing, in line with the left exhaust stack.

On the Eastern Front on the first day of the invasion of the USSR, June 22, 1941, a K5(E) sits on a Vögele turntable. From the small number of crewmen present, this photograph seems to have been taken during a lull in the action, and the men appear to be engaged in cleaning the barrel. In the right background are a mix of cars belonging to the battery.

A close-up of a K5(E) installed on the firing bed of a Vögele turntable reveals some interesting details of the rear truck, the rear part of the car body, the folding crew access ladder, and the generator housing. German railroad guns were assigned serial numbers by the Deutsche Reichsbahn, the national railway; this one was 919210.

An officer clad only in shorts and a cap stands at the top of the ladder at the left rear of a K5(E) car body. The side frame of the truck is covered with stenciled data, including an illegible Reichsbahn number. Other markings are visible, including two white squares at the rear corner of the car body and stencils identifying various fixtures.

In a battery site in 1940, most likely in France, a K5(E) with its gun barrel at or near full elevation is positioned on a Vögele turntable. It appears that the emplacement, in rugged terrain, would have been a good one to mask the gun from enemy reconnaissance aircraft. On the siding to the left is a supply car, and a flatcar is visible toward the right.

A K5(E) is in battery position in the background, in a terrain characterized by ravines and small hills. A close inspection of the photo reveals a group of personnel standing partway between the photographer and the railroad gun. In the right and left foreground are two different tracks that apparently provided access to the battery site.

On a stretch of track somewhere in Europe, a K5(E) is in firing order. The 28 cm gun barrel is elevated, and the deck panel just aft of the breech has been raised. Visible under the car body below the gun's breech is the platform of the gun-control station, with the legs of two gunners visible on it. Much stenciling is present on the car body and trucks. The tilted supports under the barrel of the gun were part of the gun's cradle assembly, and normally they were out of sight when the gun was lowered. *Thomas Anderson collection*

CHAPTER 2

The K5(E) Up Close: Surviving Examples

Many of the guns were lost during the war, either through Allied attack or deliberate destruction by the Germans to prevent their capture. Although several examples were captured, many of which were at least largely intact, today only two examples of the K5(E) are known to have survived (although rumors surface from time to time of a third example in Russia, but no evidence of this has yet surfaced). One example each of an Ausf. C and Ausf. D remain. The surviving Ausf. C was assembled for evaluation by the US Army from two partly destroyed examples captured near Anzio. Each of the K5(E) was officially named by the Germans, as well as having a Reichsbahn (German railway) number assigned, as did all other German railway equipment. The two guns captured by US troops in Civitavecchia, Italy, were 919216 ("Robert") and 919219 ("Leopold"). The two-gun battery, E.712, had been given the nickname "Anzio Express" by the Allied troops that had been faced with shelling by the guns. The Germans had begun withdrawing the guns from the Anzio area, with their ammunition supply exhausted. When the rail lines were cut by the Allies, the K5s were in essence stranded. The Germans then abandoned the guns on June 3, after first attempting to disable their elevation and breech mechanisms with charges.

US P-47 Thunderbolts of the 79th Fighter Group bombed and strafed the rail yard in Civitavecchia on June 6, 1944, although they were unaware that the two large guns were in the rail yard.

The next day, troops of the 168th Regiment entered the town and discovered the big guns in the rail yard. Shortly thereafter, technical experts from the US and Canadian armies arrived and began careful studies of the guns, the first of the type to be captured by the Allies.

By late November the decision had been made to transport one of the guns to the United States. "Leopold," by then known

Barrel elevated, a K5(E) is in position in a railroad cut. At least one source has identified this as "Leopold," of Eisenbahnbatterie 712 in Italy. Visible on the front of the forward truck, between the buffers, is the yoke for coupling the gun to the recoil mechanism of a Vögele turntable.

among GIs as "Anzio Annie," was selected for the journey, with some repairs having been made by utilizing parts from "Robert."

"Leopold" arrived in Naples, Italy, on March 15, 1945, along with its supporting train. "Leopold" traveled farther, to Taranto, where the gun tube was separated from the carriage and loaded on the deck of the Liberty ship *Robert R. Livingston*, which steamed toward New York on March 18. The support train was loaded onto other transport at Naples. *Livingston* tied up at Staten Island, New York, on July 6. The gun finally arrived at Aberdeen Proving Ground, in Maryland, in mid-September. The battery mate of "Leopold," "Robert," was apparently abandoned in Italy.

However, "Leopold" was not the only K5(E) to come to the United States. In February 1946, two more of the massive rail guns arrived at Aberdeen. One of these, K5(E) Ausf. D 919396, was a new, unissued weapon, while the other, 919214, was an experimental Glatt smoothbore weapon. By the late 1940s the two new arrivals had been reduced to scrap, and even "Leopold" was briefly offered for scrap auction in August 1949 before being withdrawn from sale upon appeal of Col. George Jarrett, director of the Ordnance Museum.

As a result of this makeshift origin and six subsequent decades on public display, today "Leopold" is missing some components.

The story of the surviving Ausf. D is a bit less certain. This weapon was stored, with few people knowing of its existence, at the French army's central artillery workshop, the Atelier de Construction at Tarbes, in the French Pyrenees. The weapon carries a builder's plate reading "Fried Krupp A.G. Essen 1941." Beyond that rudimentary information, little is known about the massive cannon—including where it came from or how it wound up in Tarbes. In the mid-1980s, the existence of the K5 became known, with various enterprises in France, England, and Germany seeking to obtain it for display. Ultimately, it was decided to loan the huge cannon to the Atlantic Wall Museum, who would display the gun adjacent to a casement of Batterie Todt at Audinghen, near Calais. The K5(E) had operated in Calais, which was one of the factors influencing the decision regarding where the piece's home would be.

The French railway would not allow the K5 to be moved by rail, and thus it was partially dismantled for transport via truck. The weapon arrived at its new home in mid-1992. Although basically in good condition, the K5 had been stored outdoors postwar, and all traces of its original markings had been lost. The museum undertook a restoration of the piece, which was in progress when the photos in this volume were taken. Since the gun was unknown, the museum was left to its own devices when it came to selecting a paint scheme. Incredibly, the museum opted to repaint the gun in spurious "Leopold" markings!

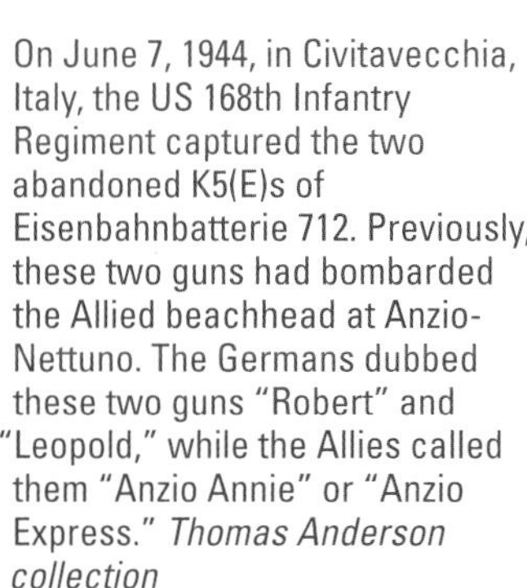

On June 7, 1944, in Civitavecchia, Italy, the US 168th Infantry Regiment captured the two abandoned K5(E)s of Eisenbahnbatterie 712. Previously, these two guns had bombarded the Allied beachhead at Anzio-Nettuno. The Germans dubbed these two guns "Robert" and "Leopold," while the Allies called them "Anzio Annie" or "Anzio Express." *Thomas Anderson collection*

A US Navy photographer shot this photo of one of the captured K5(E)s, and included in his caption is "in the heavily bombed railway yards at Civitavecchia, Italy, June 9, 1944. Note camouflage frames on the gun, which may be one of those used to shell the Anzio beaches earlier in the year. Inscription on the side of the gun car reads "Deutsche Reichsbahn Berlin 919 216." Thus, this photo is "Robert." *National Archives*

This view of "Robert" in Civitavecchia was published in TM 30-246, *Tactical Interpretation of Air Photos*, in February 1954. Notice the "R" visible on the side of the railcar—the rest of the weapon's name, which is clearly visible in earlier photos, apparently has by this point in the war been obscured by camouflage. *National Archives*

The breech end of the 28 cm gun of one of the K5(E)s captured at Civitavecchia, most likely "Leopold," is observed close-up while the gun is in transit. A notation on the photo indicates that the gun's "chamber was badly scored by acid or torch" when the US forces captured the piece. On the right of the breech is the open breechblock. To the left rear of the breech is the cartridge tray, and to the lower left is a rammer.

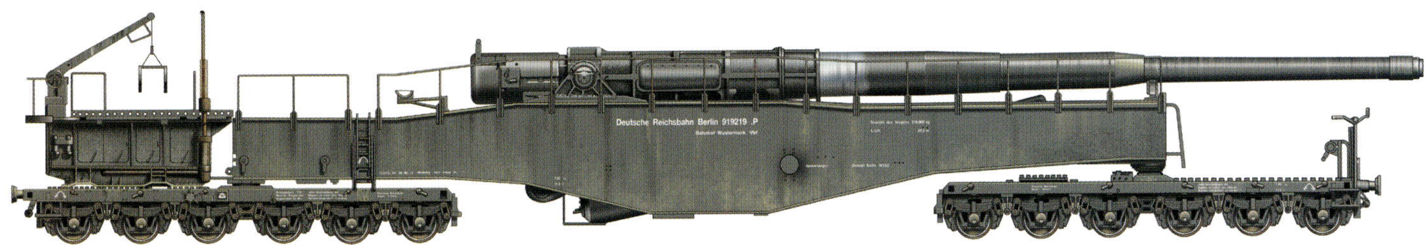

The right profile of the K5(E) railway gun that later gained fame under the name of "Leopold" and the Allied nickname "Anzio Annie" is shown in an early color scheme. Early examples of the K5(E) were painted at the factory an overall dark gray. At this point, no effort had been made to apply camouflage paint over the gray base color of this example, although some early K5(E)s had a wavy camouflage pattern of brownish paint applied over the dark-gray base color. At the top center of the car body is a white identification stencil that reads "Deutsche Reichsbahn Berlin 919219.P." This signifies that this railway gun was assigned to the Berlin division of the German national railroad system, and the individual number of the weapon was 919219. Below that inscription in smaller letters is "Bahnhof Wustermark Vbf," a reference to Wustermark Railway Station, near Berlin. Several small white stencils are present on the sides of the car body, and there is considerable stenciling on the sides of the trucks. Vertical weather streaking and dust are present on the 28 cm gun, the car, the trucks, and the generator housing mounted on the rear truck. The barrel is burnished from recoil action for several feet to the front of the sleeve of the gun cradle. The exhaust lines on the battery housing exhibit corrosion. By the time "Leopold" was captured by US troops, the weapon had been painted overall tan.

"Leopold" was photographed after its capture by US forces. The Germans had attempted to destroy both "Leopold" and "Robert" when they abandoned them, but "Leopold" was only slightly damaged when captured. The Americans cannibalized some parts from "Robert" to repair "Leopold" so that it could be tested at Aberdeen Proving Ground in Maryland. *Thomas Anderson collection*

A man inspects the breechblock mechanism of "Leopold" after its capture. The original name "Leopold," as painted in white by the Germans, appears on the right side of the car body. The vehicle and gun reportedly were painted *Dunkelgelb*, or dark yellow, when captured. The bows on top of the car body were meant to support canvas covers. *Thomas Anderson collection*

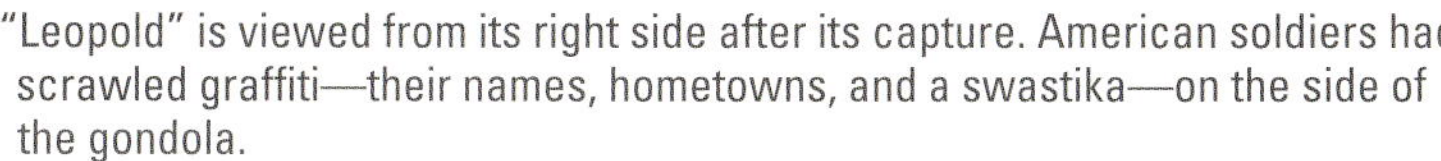
"Leopold" is viewed from its right side after its capture. American soldiers had scrawled graffiti—their names, hometowns, and a swastika—on the side of the gondola.

"Leopold" was shipped from Italy to Aberdeen Proving Ground, Maryland. The 28 cm gun tube has been secured to the main deck of a transport ship. The tube is resting on supports made of timbers, which have been secured to the deck at intervals.

K5(E) specifications		
Length of car:	95 ft., 7 in.	29.1 meters
Length of car body:	69 ft., 8 in.	21.23 meters
Width of car:	8 ft., 8½ in.	2.65 meters
Length of barrel:	70 ft., 8 in.	21.5 meters
Length of rifling:	57 ft.	14.4 meters
Rifling:	right hand	uniform twist
Number of rifling grooves:	12	
Caliber:	11.14 inches	28 cm
Weight of barrel:	187,880 lbs	85,221 kg
Barrel recoil:	32 inches	81.28 centimeters
Projectile weight:	550 pounds	249.48 kilograms
Elevation:	50 degrees	
Traverse of carriage:	½ degree	L or R
Traverse on turntable:	360 degrees	
Weight:	230 tons (460,000 lbs.)	208,652 kg

"Leopold" rests outside the Industrial Assembly and Repair Division at Aberdeen Proving Ground in October 1945, just after the division finished reconditioning and repainting the gun. While the markings accurately reproduce the originals, even at this early point in its US custody, some components are missing.

Deutsche Reichsbahn Equipment Number for 28 cm K5 series

Serial Number	Deutsche Reichsbahn Series number	Battery
1	919 201	688 & 701
2	919 210	686 & 712 & 2/725
3	919 211	
4	919 212	686
5	919 213	
6	919 214	
7	919 215	
8	919 216	712 & 2/725
9	919 217	713
10	919 218	
11	919 219	712 & 2/725
12	919 220	712
13	919 497	688
14	919 356	
15	919 396	749
16	919 397	710
17	919 398	710
18	919 399	749
19	919 400	688 & 749
20	919 443	749
21	919 444	
22	919 445	
23	919 446	
24	919 683	

"Leopold" is parked on a railroad siding next to a building at Aberdeen Proving Ground. Wooden pallets are stacked on top of the rear truck, where the generator housing normally would be mounted. The white "Leopold" inscription is visible at the center of the gondola.

In a frontal view of "Leopold" at Aberdeen, the yoke for coupling the K5(E) to the recoil mechanism of a Vögele turntable is prominent at the front. The wooden steps on the sides of the gondola have long since disappeared, but the metal supports for the steps are still intact.

The left trunnion bearing and cap, the rear of the 28 cm gun breech, the rear of the gondola, and the rear truck are seen from the left rear of "Leopold" at Aberdeen Proving Ground. Two sections of guardrails are still installed on the rear part of the gondola. Extensive white stenciling is present on the truck and the gondola.

TSgt. George H. Barrett and Sgt. David B. Dreiman, US Army, pose on the 28 cm barrel of "Leopold" after the railroad gun was delivered to Aberdeen Proving Ground. Despite suffering some damage before its capture, the weapon and railcar were in surprisingly good condition, and "Robert" had provided parts to replace damaged ones. *Greg Heuer collection*

"Leopold" is viewed from the right side. Judging from the clean and, evidently, freshly painted condition of the piece, the photo is assumed to have been taken after its initial evaluation at Aberdeen Proving Ground. The generator housing was absent from the rear truck.

"Leopold" is observed from the left rear at Aberdeen Proving Ground. The big gun, which arrived at Aberdeen in 1945, remained on outdoor display there for over six decades.

A close-up view of the rear of the breech of the 28 cm gun of "Leopold," at Aberdeen Proving Ground, also includes details of the trunnion and the cap that secured the trunnion to the trunnion bearing, to the far left.

Following its October 1945 renovation at Aberdeen Proving Ground, the markings are clearly legible, including the original-style "Leopold" inscription; the Deutsche Reichsbahn Berlin number, 919219; and "Bahnhof Wustermark Vbf" (the railroad yard, west of Berlin, that was the depot for the K5 railroad artillery pieces).

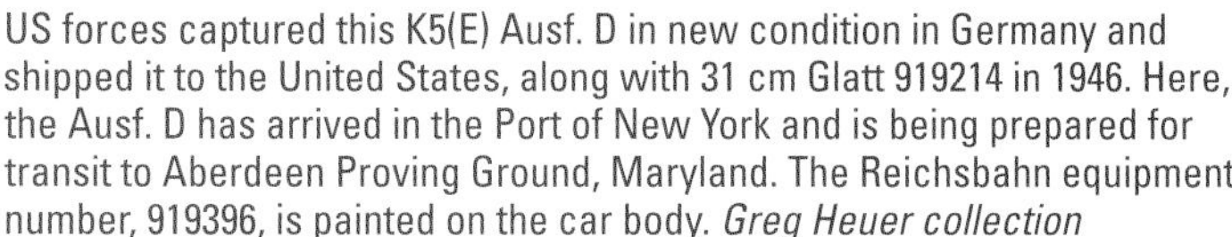

US forces captured this K5(E) Ausf. D in new condition in Germany and shipped it to the United States, along with 31 cm Glatt 919214 in 1946. Here, the Ausf. D has arrived in the Port of New York and is being prepared for transit to Aberdeen Proving Ground, Maryland. The Reichsbahn equipment number, 919396, is painted on the car body. *Greg Heuer collection*

Here, the K5(E) Ausf. D paused in a railroad yard, likely at or near Aberdeen Proving Ground. Visible on the car body is the hand-painted "SOUVENIR FROM GERMANY" and stenciled "ALLIED FORCES" markings. A cover has been tied over the muzzle of the 28 cm gun.

"Leopold," in the foreground at Aberdeen Proving Ground on February 7, 1946. Two more K5(E) railroad guns are parked on the opposite side of "Leopold," with their gun tubes pointing to the right. One of them is K5(E) Ausf. D 919396, while the other is 31 cm K5(E) Glatt 919214. The two guns in the background had just arrived at the proving ground.

The Germans modified two K5(E)s to fire the Peenemünder *Pfeilgeschosse* (Peenemünde arrow shells) by reboring the 28 cm barrel to 31 cm caliber and making it a smooth bore. These two weapons were designated the K5 Glatt. The Peenemünder *Pfeilgeschosse*, also designated the *Flugstabilisierte Treibringgeschoss*, was a high-explosive, finned, discarding-sabot projectile of 12 cm caliber and 1.9-meter length. This photograph of one of the two K5 Glatts after its capture by Allied forces shows how this railroad gun was virtually indistinguishable from the K5(E). *Ordnance Museum collection*

The K5(E) dubbed "Leopold" by the Germans and "Anzio Annie" by the beleaguered Allied troops at Anzio remained on outdoor display at Aberdeen Proving Ground until November 2010, when it was moved to its new home at the Ordnance Museum at Fort Lee, Virginia.

Two K5(E)s survive in display settings. After its capture in Italy in 1944, "Leopold," a K5(E) Ausf. C, was shipped to Aberdeen Proving Ground. Following tests there, the gun was placed on permanent display for many decades. "Leopold" has been repainted several times since its capture, and much of the extensive original stenciling on the car body and trucks has been painted over. Inauthentic camouflage schemes have also been applied from time to time.

Another surviving K5(E) is currently on display at Batterie Todt at Musée du Mur de l'Atlantique (Atlantic Wall Museum), Audinghen, Pas-de-Calais, France. This railroad gun was found in the yard of an army artillery workshop in Tarbes, France, in 1980. The gun was produced by Krupp in 1941, but the background of this K5(E) Ausf. D is obscure. It is possible it was assigned to Eisenbahnbatterie 749 and abandoned when the Allies advanced up the Rhône valley late in the war. In the background is Tower 1, or Turm 1, a huge casemate that once housed a 380 mm naval gun and now serves as the museum. *Pierre-Olivier Buan*

Viewed from the front, the stepped construction of the 28 cm gun barrel of "Leopold" is apparent. The twelve grooves of the right-hand, uniform-twist rifling, 7 mm deep, are visible on the gun.

The front of the front truck of "Leopold" exhibits a number of details. The round buffers on both sides of the truck were a component in the European style of coupling cars, to keep the cars from banging together.

This massive, swiveling yoke mounted on the front of the front truck of the K5(E)s, when folded down, served as the coupling point for the firing bed's recoil mechanism on the Vögele turntables.

The right front buffer of "Leopold" is viewed close-up. Along the side frames of the front truck are brackets for wooden steps, the planks of which are now missing. The lower bracket was hinged so the step could be folded.

Visible in this frontal view of the left front buffer of "Leopold" are the thick pins that secure the recoil mechanism yoke to eyes on the forward side of the front truck.

The K5(E)s used buffer-and-chain couplers, the chains being the turnbuckle-screw type. At the center is the towing hook, with a chain link pinned to each side of it. The rearward-facing idler hook is below the towing hook.

The chain seen here on the K5(E) at Batterie Todt is more complete than the one surviving on "Leopold." The U-shaped link at the end of the chain would be attached to the hook of an adjoining locomotive or car, and the turnbuckle would then be tightened until the buffers touched each other. *Pierre-Olivier Buan*

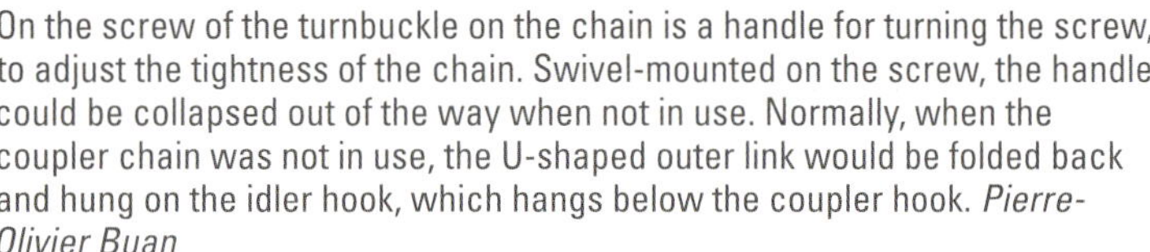

On the screw of the turnbuckle on the chain is a handle for turning the screw, to adjust the tightness of the chain. Swivel-mounted on the screw, the handle could be collapsed out of the way when not in use. Normally, when the coupler chain was not in use, the U-shaped outer link would be folded back and hung on the idler hook, which hangs below the coupler hook. *Pierre-Olivier Buan*

The coupler chain on the front of the front truck of the Batterie Todt K5(E) is viewed from the left. The two large holes of different sizes on the recoil yoke accepted strong steel pins that secured the yoke to the recuperator and buffer of the recoil mechanism. A small latch on the column at the center of the deck on top of the truck holds the yoke in its stored position. *Pierre-Olivier Buan*

As viewed from the right front corner of the Batterie Todt K5(E), details of the coupler chain and hook are visible. At the bottom edge of the front frame of the truck, on either side of the hook, are brake-line fittings with shutoff valves. *Pierre-Olivier Buan*

This view shows some of the elements of the suspension at the front of the front truck of "Leopold." To the left is the upper yoke of the idler hook, the purpose of which was to support the coupler chain when not in use.

The front bumpers of the front truck of "Leopold" are viewed from the right side. They are secured with locking nuts to the front frame of the truck. Between the buffers is the recoil yoke, with the coupler hook protruding through it.

To the right of center is the front edge of the front right wheel of "Leopold." In front of the edge of the wheel, the brake shoe and brake hanger are visible. There is a brake shoe on each side of the first, second, fifth, and sixth wheels.

The front truck is viewed from the front right corner. The objects attached to each top corner of the frame on top of the front of the truck served to hold lanterns or placards. The frame also supported a hand brake, not present here.

The frame atop the front of the front truck is shown on "Leopold." On the stand at center is a hand winch, the cable from which raised and lowered the recoil yoke, to the right of center.

The hand winch is viewed from the rear left, showing how the frame of the winch is bolted to the rear side of a stand made from an I beam. To the right is a sign added as part of the museum display.

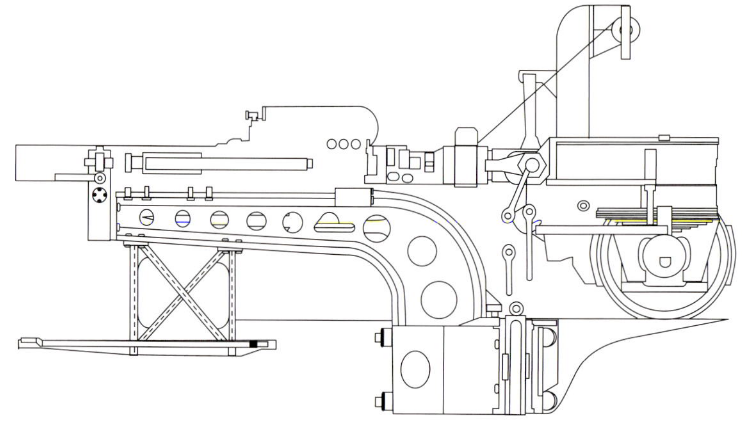

Turntable Recoil Unit

To support the enormous weight of the K5(E), each truck (*Drehgestelle* in German parlance) had six wheels per side, 900 mm in diameter, each on its own leaf-spring suspension. Above the truck looms the front of the car body.

The wheels are suspended on semielliptic leaf springs, each having ten leaves. Below the access hole is the oval-shaped front spring shackle. Below the spring is the journal box, the plain bearing on which the wheel rotates.

A journal box (or *Achslager*) cover is viewed close-up. Cast on its cover is the maker's mark, Schütte, Meyer & Co., of Letmathe, Germany, dated 1939.

The front right journal box of "Leopold" is viewed from the front, showing how the cover is fastened to the box with bolts and locking nuts. Seen close-up to the far right is the front brake shoe of the front right wheel.

Another of the journal box covers of "Leopold" is shown together with the corresponding leaf spring assembly, comprising ten leaves. Above the journal box cover is a locking device for immobilizing the spring when the gun is fired.

Shackle mountings are viewed from an angle. The nuts securing the shackles to their mounts are locked in place with cotter pins. To the lower left is a journal box and cover, viewed from the side.

A brake shoe is viewed diagonally, with the brake beam visible to the left of it. The brake beam was connected to a brake shoe on each side of the truck; a lever exerted pressure on the beam to actuate the brakes.

The lower right-rear corner of the front truck of "Leopold" is depicted. Toward the bottom of the cover of the journal box is a filler and cap for lubricant for the packing material in the box. To the left is the rearmost brake beam of the truck.

Details of the lower right-rear corner of the front truck are present in this view taken from directly to the rear. At the center of the photo are the brake and its hanger, while toward the bottom is the brake beam.

Visible here are elements of the brake rigging (*Bremsgestänge*), the mechanical assemblies that transfer force from the brake cylinders or hand brakes to the brake shoes. Running horizontally above the brake beam at the rear of the front truck of "Leopold" is a shaft with turnbuckle, by which the brake hangers were adjusted. The drum-shaped object left of center is an air reservoir for the brake system.

The air reservoir seen in the photograph at left is shown here close-up. It is suspended from the underside of the truck platform by heavy-duty metal straps. To the right are details of the brake rigging.

A view of the inside of the right-rear wheel of the front truck of "Leopold" shows the rear left brake, brake hanger, and U-shaped guard, made of rod. To the top is the left side of the turnbuckle for adjusting the brake hangers.

The rear brake on the left side of the front truck of "Leopold" is viewed close-up at the center of the photo. The brake shoe is on a pivot mount between the two upright supports with the small coil spring between them.

“Leopold” is viewed from its front right side. Eisenbahnbatterie 712 dealt havoc to the Allied invasion forces at Anzio, Italy, with this weapon and its brother K5(E), nicknamed “Robert.” “Leopold” was assigned Reichsbahn number 919219.

A right-rear view of "Leopold" shows the design of its rear truck. This relic lacks the generator housing on the rear truck. Like the front truck, the rear truck had six axles. On the rear frame of the truck are two buffers.

Unlike "Leopold," the K5(E) Ausf. D at Batterie Todt, Musée du Mur de l'Atlantique (Atlantic Wall Museum), Audinghen, France, has a relatively complete generator housing. Powered by a Maybach diesel engine, the Ward-Leonard generator supplied electricity for operating systems on the gun mount, including the electric elevation drive, and on the trucks. When the K5(E) was on a Vögele turntable, the generator also provided electricity to the firing bed. The ammunition crane and an ammunition trolley are visible on top of the generator housing. *Pierre-Olivier Buan*

The front of the rear truck (bogie) of the K5(E) at Batterie Todt is viewed from the right side. A built-in ladder is at the center of the rear frame of the truck. This K5(E) has suffered heavy deterioration from exposure to the elements. *Pierre-Olivier Buan*

The crew ladder is seen in this frontal view of the rear truck of "Leopold." To the rear of the ladder are the brake beam, brake lever, and, up against the rear edges of the rear wheels, both of the rear brakes.

The front right corner of the rear truck of "Leopold" is illustrated. The hook welded to the corner plate was to hold a chain, the other end of which was attached to the car body, to keep these vehicles in line in the event of a derailment.

Looming above the front right corner of the rear truck of "Leopold" is the car body. The front of the rear truck and the rear of the front truck were not fitted with buffers, since there were no provisions for coupling these ends of the trucks.

The lever above the triangular-shaped eye is a hand lever for locking the mechanism for blocking the suspension springs during firing.

The wheel below the triangular eye was another part of the mechanism for blocking the springs when the gun was fired. *Pierre-Olivier Buan*

A spoked handwheel is mounted on the fitting aft of the triangular eye on the Batterie Todt K5(E). *Pierre-Olivier Buan*

As seen on the Batterie Todt K5(E), the handwheel was fabricated by welding metal bars to a central disk. *Pierre-Olivier Buan*

Visible in this view of the right rear of the rear truck of "Leopold" are step brackets (missing their wooden plank steps), as well as the rear journal box, spring shackle, and rounded square access hole on the side frame.

At the bottom of the rear frame of the rear truck of "Leopold," next to the right buffer, is a coupler for brake air. An air pipe is fastened to the coupler. The shutoff lever is on the right side of the coupler.

At the rear of the rear truck of the Batterie Todt K5(E), an air brake hose is dangling from the face of the truck, at the right in the photo. *Pierre-Olivier Buan*

As seen from the left rear of the rear truck of "Leopold," the track on the deck of the truck was to guide the left rollers of the generator housing when that structure was hauled onto the truck or rolled off it.

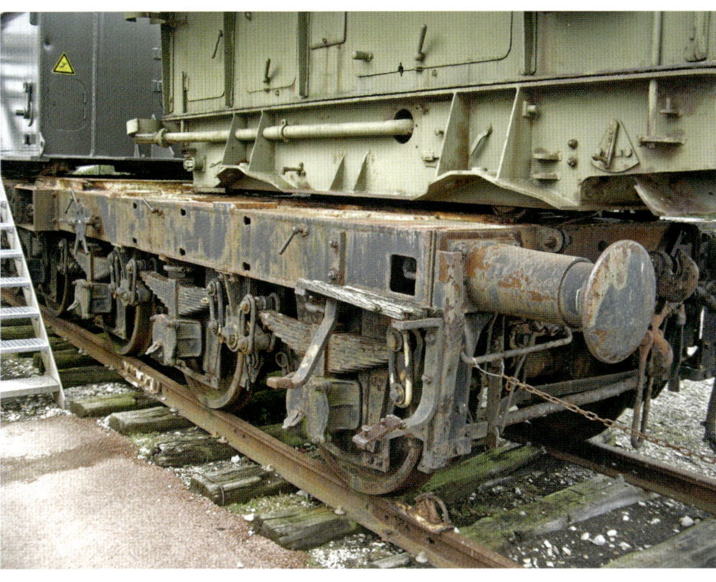

Rising above the left rear of the rear truck of the K5(E) on display at Batterie Todt is the generator housing, painted a light-green color. The pipe issuing through the hole in it is what remains of the exhaust. *Pierre-Olivier Buan*

The rear wheel and journal box of the rear truck are displayed. The journal box cover bears the maker's mark of Knorr-Bremse, a major German manufacturer of railroad equipment, founded in Berlin in 1905. *Pierre-Olivier Buan*

The left rear of the rear truck of the Batterie Todt K5 (E) is viewed from a different angle. All that remained of the crew-access steps when photographed were parts of the frames and a rotting top step. *Pierre-Oliver Buan*

In this view of the left rear wheel and journal box on the rear truck of "Leopold," the step planks are missing, and the hinges for the lower step are shown raised, as they would have been when the K5(E) was in transit, to provide side clearance.

The second-from-rear wheel on the right side of the rear truck of "Leopold" is at the center. In this area of the truck, a platform would have been hung over the side frame for the electricians to stand on when necessary.

Below the handwheel with the missing handle is the third wheel from the rear on the rear truck of the Batterie Todt K5(E). Toward the lower right is a close-up view of the side of a brake shoe, with a torsion spring attached to it. *Pierre-Olivier Buan*

On each truck, the rear of the spring of the third wheel from the front, and the front of the spring of the fourth wheel, are shackled to a frame-type bracket. This one is at the left center of the rear truck of "Leopold."

The point where the freshly painted car body of the Batterie Todt K5(E) is mounted to the top of the rear truck is at the center of the photo. A towing/lifting eye and three access doors are visible at the rear of the car body. *Pierre-Olivier Buan*

A wheel on each side of the underside of the rear of the car body (*center*) rested on a circular track on the top deck of the truck, to help the trucks bear the enormous weight of the car and gun and to enhance the stability of the vehicle on curves.

This panel at the center of the left side of the rear truck, the counterpart of the box shown with its cover installed in the preceding photo of "Leopold," appears to have contained hydraulic gauges. *Pierre-Olivier Buan*

The corresponding hydraulic gauge box is shown on "Leopold." The top of the cover was hinged to the top of the box, and the bottom of the cover was secured shut with two toggle bolts and wing nuts.

Just forward of the box on the left side of the rear truck of "Leopold" is a selector switch for the Hildebrand-Knorr air-brake system's automatic brake distributor. The "GUT.Z" and "PERS.Z" on the control refer, respectively, to freight-car and passenger-car settings.

A diagonal view along the wheels and suspension on the left side of the rear truck of "Leopold" reveals various details of the brakes, leaf springs, spring shackles, spring brackets, and journal boxes. Cotter pins were used to lock the various nuts.

An uncoupled air hose dangles in this view under the car body of "Leopold," facing forward from the left side of the vehicle. Visible under the center of the body are the bottom of the gun cradle and the rear of the equilibrator of the elevation mechanism.

Flanking the kingpin of the front truck of "Leopold" (*center*), seen from the rear, are rollers fixed to the top of the truck, bearing on the underside of the car body. The fixture to the far left and its counterpart on the other side of the K5(E) appear to have been traverse indicators.

At the left rear of the front truck of "Leopold" is safety chain, which would help limit damage in a derailment. Although the markings on Leopold are replicas, "DESSART" was the acronym for *Deutsche sehr schwere Artillerie* (German very heavy artillery).

The left rear wheel of the front truck of "Leopold" is shown, including the distinctive rear spring bracket. The journal box is suspended between the journal box guides, which kept the axle longitudinally stable while allowing it to move vertically against the springs to compensate for track conditions.

The side frame of the left side of the front truck of "Leopold" is viewed up close. Various oblong and rectangular cutouts are present on the top decks of the trucks. The bodies of the trucks are of welded construction. The gauge of the steel may be seen at the cutouts.

The casting toward the left is the gearbox of the traversing system, for making minute traverse adjustments by moving the car body's mounting 6 inches, or about 1 degree, either way of the center of the mount. An electric motor inside the truck drove the gearbox.

The gearbox is viewed from straight on, displaying its rough-cast texture and the presence of a casting number. Mounted near the bottom of the side frame of the truck is the selector switch for the automatic brake distributor for the front truck.

The plate fitted around the front end of the gearbox was the operating panel, where the traversing mechanism on the front truck could be manually operated and locked if necessary. Usually, the gunner controlled traverse from the gun control station.

The operating panel on the K5(E) at Batterie Todt is in an advanced state of deterioration, but several parts lacking on "Leopold" are present here, including a data or manufacturer's plate at the center, a retainer chain, and two steel clips. *Pierre-Olivier Buan*

The operating panel is hinged at the front. Toward the upper left is the front of the mounting for the car body. Not visible behind the girder structure on the truck is the driveshaft linking the gearbox to the sliding traverse mechanism to the far left.

The roller on the right side of the front truck of "Leopold" is viewed from the outside of the truck. The two rollers on the front truck helped support the car body and facilitated its movement when the K5(E) was proceeding on curved stretches of track.

The right roller and its bracket on the front truck of "Leopold" are viewed from the front. It is attached to the top deck of the truck with lock nuts secured with cotter pins. To the rear of the bracket is the indicator and its associated linkage.

Visible from the right side of the front truck of "Leopold" is the slide mechanism on which the front mount for the car body moved from side to side, to effect the fine-tuning of the 28 cm gun's traverse. To the top is the front of the car body.

The forward part of the front truck of "Leopold" is viewed from the left side, showing details of the upper deck and side frame. To the front center of the deck is the hand winch on an I-beam support, aft of which is a museum display sign.

The front of the "Leopold" car body is viewed from the left side of the front truck. A crew access ladder is on each side, and three access doors are present. Dangling from the front of the car is piping for compressed air. Atop the front of the car is the gun travel lock.

On the left-side frame of the front truck of "Leopold" is a sheet-metal board with a tubular frame with woven wire in the manner of chicken wire. This was a holder for a transport authorization form. The frame was hinged at the top.

A view across the deck of the front truck from the right side reveals further details of the compressed air line and another section of air line fastened to the side of the oblong opening in the foreground. Another air line with shutoff valve is in the adjacent opening.

In a view looking down at the deck of the front truck, facing aft, in the center opening is a brake cylinder and pushrod. Two brake cylinders are present on each of the trucks. The Hildebrand-Knorr air-brake system was employed on the K5(E).

The front of the mounting for the car body atop the front truck of "Leopold" is viewed looking downward, with the front of the car body to the top. To the far left is a roller bracket, and toward the right are the couplers of the two sections of air hose.

The center and left side of the front of the car body are emphasized in this shot. The center access door has been welded shut; its two hinges are toward the left side of the car body, while the hinges of the smaller access door are on the inboard side of the door.

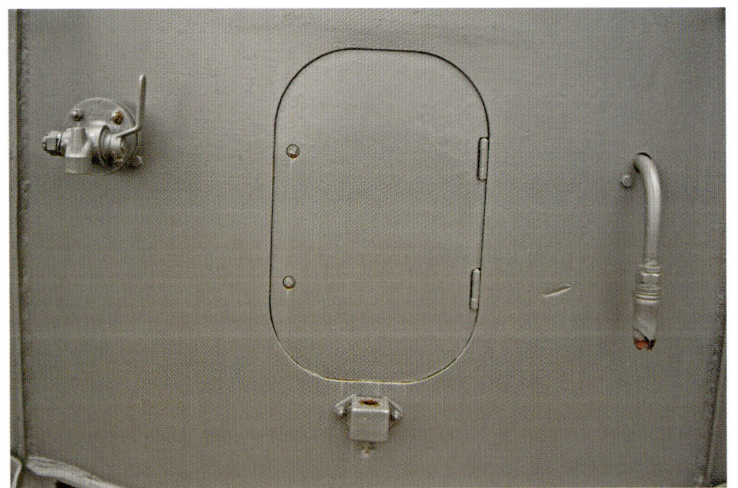

The center access door on the front of the car body of the K5(E) at Batterie Todt is shown. On the edge of the door, opposite the hinges, are two square bolt heads to operate internal latches. To the sides of the door are an air pipe and a coupler with shutoff handle. *Pierre-Olivier Buan*

The focus here is on the right access door and crew ladder. The top of the ladder is secured to two eyes welded to the car body with a hinge pin. At the top of the car body is the front of the 28 cm gun's travel lock, with timbers placed on it to hold the gun barrel. *Pierre-Olivier Buan*

The travel lock is shown close-up from the front. Originally, when the gun was secured for transit, the two curved retainers were swung over the barrel and secured with a pin. The wooden blocks apparently were placed under the barrel to hold it at a desired angle. *Pierre-Olivier Buan*

The right retainer on the travel lock of "Leopold" is badly bent. It is also of a different design from the same part on the Batterie Todt K5(E) in the photo above, The left retainer is broken off. The cushion on the cradle of the travel lock is now mostly missing.

The travel lock on "Leopold" is seen from aft. The right retainer would be secured to the left retainer with the toggle bolt. The nuts that fasten the travel lock to the deck of the car body are secured by thin metal lock washers on which the edges were bent upward.

The travel lock of "Leopold" is viewed from farther aft. In the foreground is an access panel with a grab handle on each side, and two wing nuts on each side to secure the panel in place. The frame at the front of the front truck is visible in the distance.

In a view facing toward the rear from the left side of the forward deck of the car body of "Leopold," in the foreground an access panel has been removed, but three access panels remain in place. One of the access panels features two protrusions on top to provide clearance to the elevation gears.

Unlike the access panels on the forward deck of "Leopold," these panels on the Batterie Todt K5(E) are secured with turn latches, including two on each side of the panel with the protrusions. These panels are made from fairly thin-gauge sheet metal. *Pierre-Olivier Buan*

The forward deck and the 28 cm gun barrel of the K5(E) at Batterie Todt are seen from the front right corner of the car body. The barrel features a highly pronounced step. In the distance, beyond the guardrail, is the front of the right trunnion. *Pierre-Olivier Buan*

The travel lock for the gun and the access panels on the forward deck of the Batterie Todt K5(E) are seen from the rear panel, facing forward. Running longitudinally down the deck on both sides of the access panels are weld seams. *Pierre-Olivier Buan*

With one of the access panels absent on the deck of "Leopold," part of the 28 cm gun's elevation machinery is visible below. The elevation mechanism was electrically powered by the Ward-Leonard generator in the housing mounted on the rear truck.

In the well aft of the access plates on the front deck, facing forward, the two elevation gears are visible. The segmental spur-gear rack machined into the bottom surfaces of these slat-like structures engages pinion gears to move the elevation mechanism forward and aft.

The slide, aft ends of the elevation gears, elevation equilibrator, and front ends of the elevation rods are viewed facing to the rear on the K5(E) at Batterie Todt. The trunnions of the cylinder are secured to a transverse bulkhead of the car body. *Pierre-Olivier Buan*

The slide of the elevation mechanism of "Leopold" is at the bottom, with the gun cradle to the top. A piston rod from the equilibrator, the cylinder aft of the slide, is also linked to the slide. Trunnion mounts on the sides of the equilibrator are visible.

The rear of the elevation gear (*foreground, facing aft*) is connected to a slide mounted on the track with lightening holes. Also affixed to the slide are two rods, connected to the bottom of the gun carriage. The movement of these rods actuated the gun's elevation.

The front of the sleeve of the cradle of the 28 cm gun of "Leopold" is viewed from the right front, with the right trunnion in the background. The large "disc" below the sleeve is the recuperator cylinder, flanked by two recoil buffer cylinders.

The right side of the sleeve of the cradle of the K5(E) at Batterie Todt is in view, showing the recoil buffer cylinder (the front end of which is painted red) and the right hydropneumatic cylinder. The rough texture of the sleeve casting is evident. *Pierre-Olivier Buan*

On the side of the sleeve of the gun cradle is a large, removable panel, fastened at the top and bottom to a raised flange on the sleeve. Removing this panel provided access to the side of the barrel. Further details of the recuperator and right buffer are in view. *Pierre-Olivier Buan*

The front of the right trunnion is viewed close-up. The front of the cap of the trunnion is secured to the base with two large hex screws and one smaller one. Fastened to the front of the trunnion base is a grab handle. A step with diamond tread is atop the cap.

The breech, breechblock, right trunnion, and cradle are viewed from the right side of the car body of the K5(E) at Batterie Todt. The square object on the side of the breech is the right side of the breechblock. On the side of the car body, the outlines of the interior framing members are visible, including those radiating from below the trunnion. These internal frames were essential for absorbing the tremendous shocks of firing the 28 cm gun, as well as bearing the gun's tremendous weight—approximately 94 US tons. *Pierre-Olivier Buan*

The right trunnion is viewed from the rear. Two of the three hex screws of the trunnion cap are missing. The step on top of the cap was helpful to crewmen in climbing over the trunnion, since there were only a few inches of walkway to the side of the trunnion. *Pierre-Olivier Buan*

Details of the right side of the breech (*left*), the right trunnion, and the sleeve of the gun cradle are in view. The smooth surface of the breech, as contrasted to the rough texture of the cradle sleeve, is apparent. Screwed to the trunnion cap is a curved guard. *Pierre-Olivier Buan*

A feature present on "Leopold" that is lacking on the K5(E) at Batterie Todt (refer to the preceding photo) is the network of lines neatly fastened to the gun cradle sleeve, routed up to the terminal fastened to the rib on top of the sleeve.

A series of steel bars are welded to the breech and the cradle sleeve of "Leopold." These bars were apparently added after the gun's capture and subsequent Aberdeen Proving Ground evaluation by the Americans. The step atop the left trunnion cap is visible.

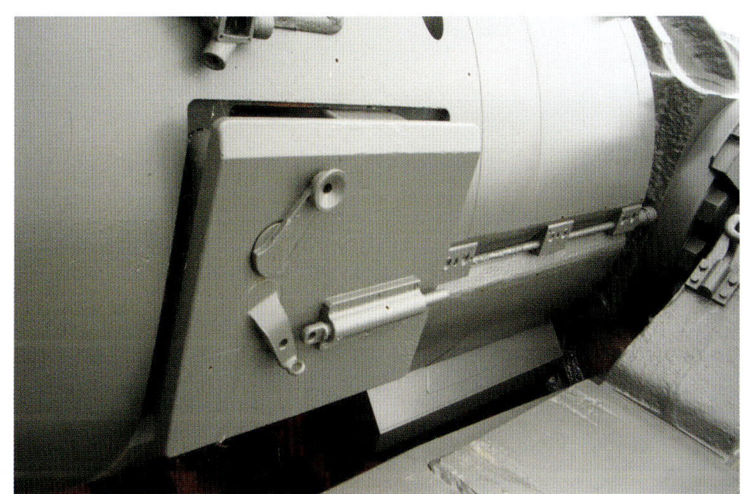

The right side of the breechblock of the K5(E) at Batterie Todt appears to be slightly open. The breechblock was of the horizontal, sliding type. Firing of the gun was by means of pulling a lanyard, triggering a percussion ignition mechanism. *Pierre-Olivier Buan*

The breechblock was operated by means of a hand crank attached to the shaft protruding from the side of the gearbox on the upper right side of the breech. The crank is not installed on the breech of the K5(E) on display at Batterie Todt, Musée du Mur de l'Atlantique. *Pierre-Olivier Buan*

The cover of the breech-operating gearbox on "Leopold" has been removed for some time, and as a result the gears are highly corroded. The crank is present, with its collapsible handle. It took one and a half rotations of the crank to open or close the breechblock.

The rear face of the breech of the 28 cm Kanone 5 presents a flat surface with rounded outer edges, as well as rounded edges around the aperture. Various inscriptions and proof marks are finely inscribed on the rear face of the breech. The cartridge tray is to the left. *Pierre-Olivier Buan*

The 28 cm gun of the K5(E) at Batterie Todt silently holds watch over the English Channel. The cartridge tray is to the left, swung into position to the rear of the breech. The tray is attached to a pivoting arm that is mounted to a stand bolted to the deck. *Pierre-Olivier Buan*

This panel, called the *Ladeklappe*, to the rear of the breech of the 28 cm gun was raised, the front end swinging up, when the gun was loaded and ready for firing. A stop is attached to each side toward the front end of the panel, and the right stop has a latch.

The right-hand stop of the lifting section of deck aft of the breech is shown up close. To the front of the stop is a grab handle fashioned from bent rod stock. Also present on this panel is a guide track for the ammunition trolley and reinforcing strips.

On the deck immediately aft of the display projectile on "Leopold" is an oval access panel. Running alongside the panel are guide tracks for the ammunition trolley. Gone is the wooden planking that originally covered this part of the deck atop the car body.

The 28 cm K5 gun used several types of projectile. They had cast-iron splines that engaged the rifling grooves of the barrel. This example displayed on the deck of "Leopold" appears to be a 28 cm Granate 35. Originally, it would have been painted *Dunkelgrau* (dark gray).

A section of guardrail is installed on the mounting brackets along the deck of "Leopold," at the right-rear side of the car body.

The guardrails are fastened to the mounting brackets with bent pins. These are fitted with retainer chains, to prevent their loss.

The slotted tab on the guardrail was for attaching a guard chain when the generator housing was not mounted behind the car.

The guardrails on the left side of the car body had a gap to allow access to the crew access ladder, the top of which is just visible, just beyond the third stanchion from the left.

This fixture on the deck of the car body, aft of the cartridge tray stand, is a storage tray for a metal rammer. The rammer would be installed on a stand next to the left side of the breechblock, to jar the breechblock loose should it become jammed.

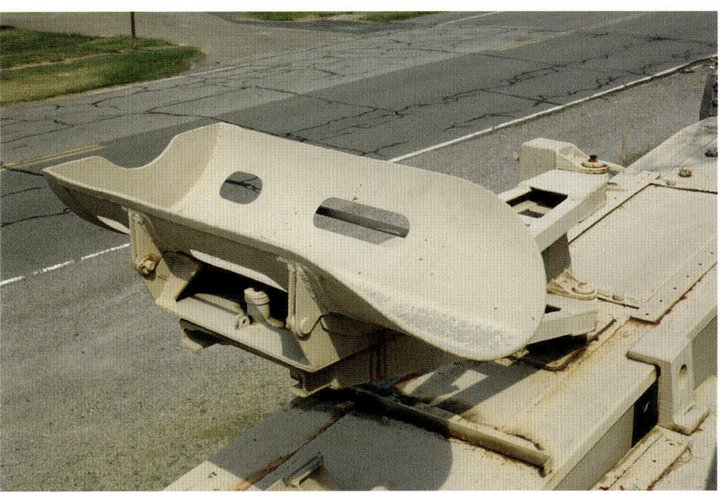

The cartridge tray on "Leopold" is viewed up close. The tray was swung behind the breech aperture after firing, and the empty cartridge was ejected onto the tray. A loader would then swing the tray to the side, pick up the cartridge, and toss it overboard.

The cartridge tray of "Leopold" is viewed from another angle. The stand for the rammer for jarring the breechblock loose when jammed is not present on "Leopold." The four lock nuts on the deck (toward the top center of the photo) mark the location where that stand would have been mounted.

The cartridge tray on the 28 cm K5(E) at Batterie Todt is deployed in the position behind the breech aperture. The supporting stand of the tray is fastened to the deck with bolts and lock nuts. The grab handle on the tray was used for tilting the tray on its hinges. *Pierre-Olivier Buan*

This is a loader's-eye view of the cartridge tray in position. The tray itself is mounted on a turntable, allowing the tray to be swung around on the support arm. The horizontal rod on the support arm has a threaded turnbuckle near the support stand. *Pierre-Olivier Buan*

On the deck of the 28 cm K5(E) at Batterie Todt, the stand and rammer for dealing with a jammed breechblock are installed. The rammer slid on guides on top of the stand. Present on the rammer are two long grab handles and two lifting eyes. *Pierre-Olivier Buan*

With the breechblock rammer in the foreground, the left trunnion is displayed. It is basically the reverse image of the right trunnion, complete with diamond-tread step on top, grab handles, and curved guard with stiffener ribs next to the gun cradle. *Pierre-Olivier Buan*

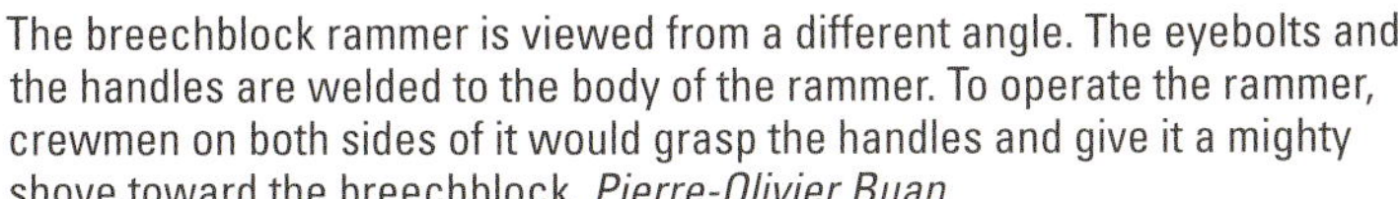

The breechblock rammer is viewed from a different angle. The eyebolts and the handles are welded to the body of the rammer. To operate the rammer, crewmen on both sides of it would grasp the handles and give it a mighty shove toward the breechblock. *Pierre-Olivier Buan*

The left side of the sleeve of the gun cradle is in the foreground. In the well below are the two elevation gears; behind the bulkhead through which they pass is the elevation machinery. Brackets for guardrails are along the side of the platform.

The left trunnion on the K5(E) at Batterie Todt is viewed from the rear, straight on. The two large hex screws on the trunnion cap are present, but the center screw with the smaller hex head is missing. Below the step is a small eyebolt. *Pierre-Olivier Buan*

To change the railroad gun from transport mode to firing mode, the rear truck was moved backward 6 feet and resecured to the car body. The entire left side of "Leopold" is seen here with the rear truck in the firing-mode position.

An extension ladder is attached to the left side of the car body of "Leopold."

The ladder has three sections. The hooks were for stowing the collapsed ladder.

The brace could be released, allowing the ladder to lie flat against car body.

Swiveling hooks on the ladder hold the lower sections when raised.

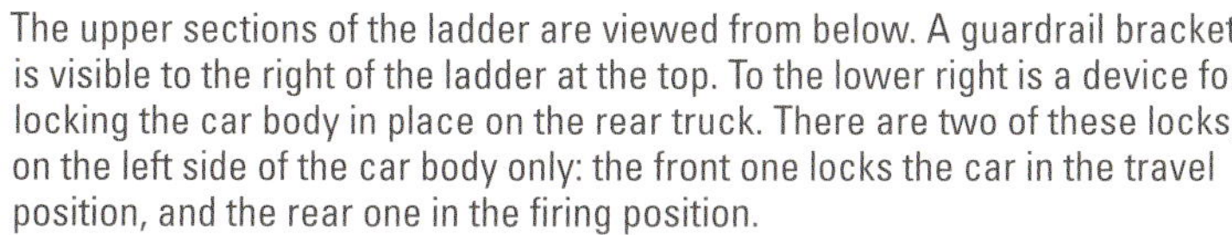

The upper sections of the ladder are viewed from below. A guardrail bracket is visible to the right of the ladder at the top. To the lower right is a device for locking the car body in place on the rear truck. There are two of these locks, on the left side of the car body only: the front one locks the car in the travel position, and the rear one in the firing position.

The lock was turned with a large wrench and secured in a bracket with the pin with the retaining chain: pinning the lock to the lower bracket locked the car in place. When the lock was pinned to the upper bracket, the device was unlocked. On "Leopold" when these photos were taken, both locks were secured in the down, or locked, positions.

The rear locking device for the car body is near the rear of the body. The "arm" of the lock is in the down, or locked, position and is pinned to the locking bracket. The bracket for securing the lock in the unlocked position is visible above the lock, with a hole in it to accommodate the retainer pin.

This is the location of the gun control station, or aiming stand, on the left side of the car body, below the trunnion, of the K5(E) Ausf. D at Batterie Todt. The instruments and controls are now missing. The control station on the Ausf. D was higher than that of the Ausf. C, of which "Leopold" is an example. *Pierre-Olivier Buan*

The top cover of the gun control station of "Leopold," which originally had hinges on the top, has been immobilized with welded brackets. This was the travel position of the cover. When the gun was deployed for firing, the cover was raised and a removable platform was installed for the gunners to stand on.

The device on the left side of the car body, below the name "Leopold," was an indicator that was swung down next to a ruler affixed to the track before firing, to measure the length of the vehicle's recoil. This way, the gunners could compensate for the movement of the gun upon firing or move the vehicle back to the exact initial position.

This access plate on the left side of the car body of "Leopold" provided access to the connections of the elevation equilibrator and the elevation gears, for lubrication and maintenance. There is a corresponding access plate on the right side of the car body. The plates are secured with eight flat-headed slotted screws.

These two levers toward the front end of the left side of the car body actuated the brakes of the elevation mechanism in the event the equilibrator failed. The elevation brakes normally operated electrically.

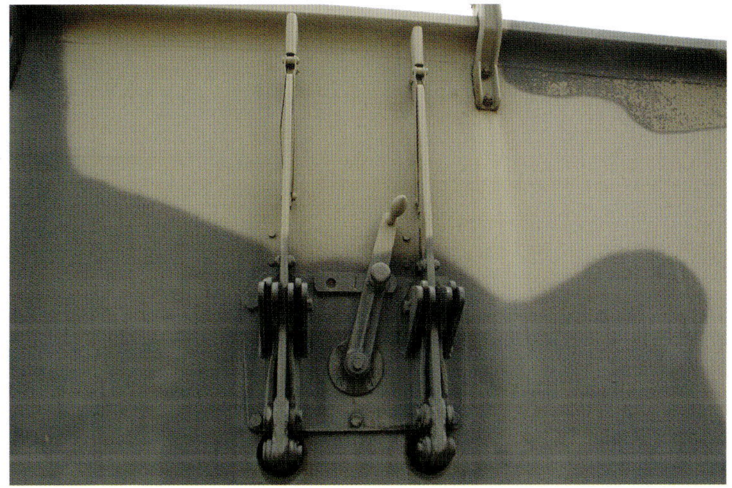

The manual brake levers for the elevation mechanism are viewed from straight on, showing the smaller lever or switch located between the brake levers. This lever features an upper handle and a smaller knob.

On the forward left side of the car body is a circular plate with two elongated ventilation holes that doubled as grab handles. The plate could be removed to allow access to the elevation mechanism compartment toward the front of the car body. The access plate and the manual elevation brake levers are shown relative to each other on the K5(E) at Batterie Todt. *Pierre-Olivier Buan*

From the platform at the rear of the car body of "Leopold," the top of the rear truck is visible. In the square opening at the center is one of the two brake cylinders of the truck. The eight small slots outboard of the two tracks were for securing the generator housing.

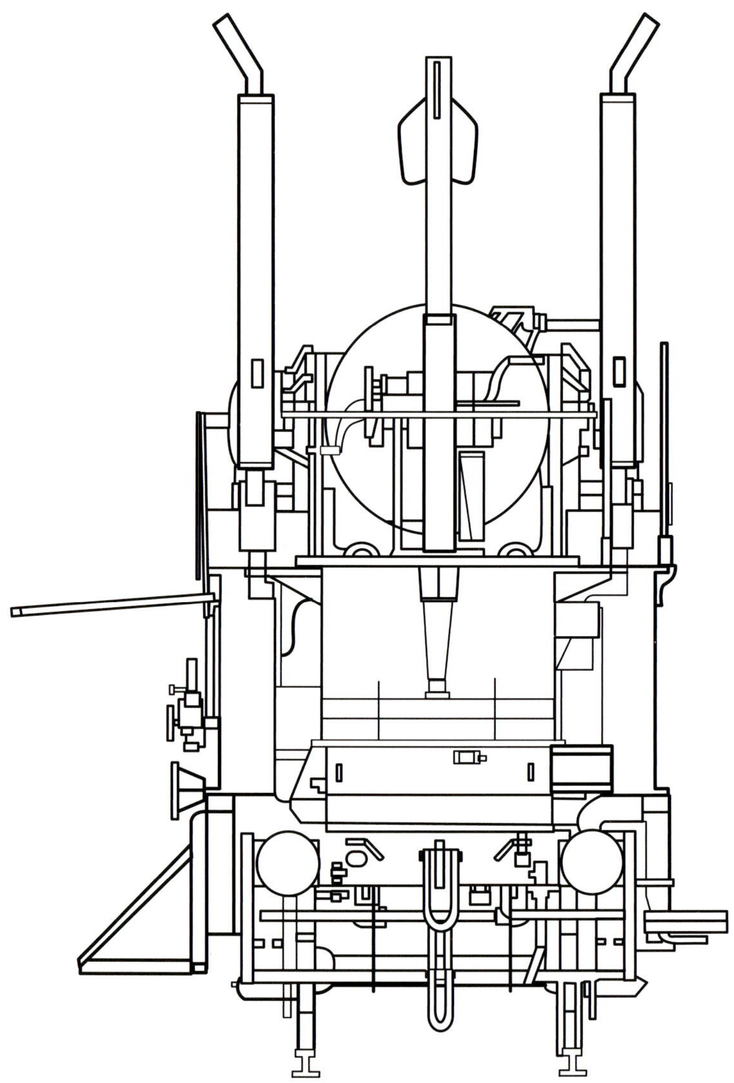

Rear View
The ammunition crane, platform, and guardrail at the rear of the roof of the generator housing of the K5(E) are in view. For structural strength and stability, the bottom of the crane extended down to a bearing on the crossbeam.

The conical shape of the lower extension of the ammunition crane and the bearing that holds it to the crossbeam are shown close-up. The crane platform has grille flooring. A sizable hole is present on the housing next to the crane bearing. *Pierre-Olivier Buan*

The right side of the generator housing of the K5(E) at Batterie Todt is exhibited. Access doors line the side of the housing. An ammunition trolley is on the roof. Of the exhaust system, only the lower, horizontal pipe is still present. *Pierre-Olivier Buan*

A short ladder originally was at the right-rear corner of the generator housing (located to the left of the photo). The platform at the top of the photo was hinged so it could be lifted during transit, and it originally had wood planks, which are now missing. *Pierre-Olivier Buan*

The forward end of the right side of the generator housing is pictured. During transit, this housing was carried on an ammunition supply car (*Munitionszubringerwagen*). At the firing site, the housing was jacked up and rolled on rails onto the rear truck. *Pierre-Olivier Buan*

In this view of the front right corner of the generator housing, the supports of the work platform on top of the housing are visible. Power cables from the generator were fed through the open doors on front of the housing, to the rear of the car body. *Pierre-Olivier Buan*

The door at the center of the rear of the car leads to the rear compartment of the car body and an opening through which electrical cables were routed from the generator to the car body. Visible here is the circular track atop the truck, as well as some puncture damage to the end of the car body. *Pierre-Olivier Buan*

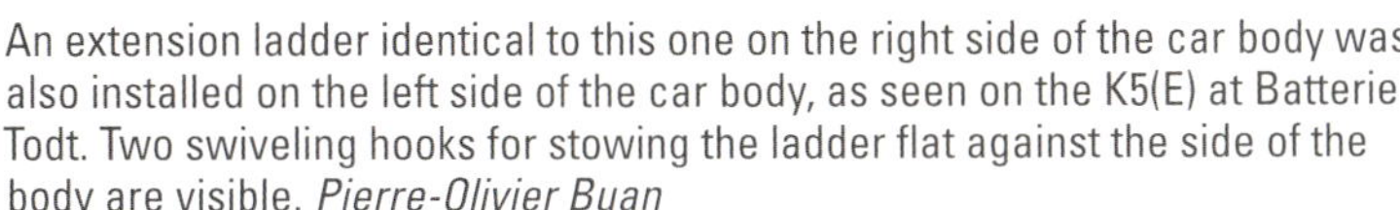

An extension ladder identical to this one on the right side of the car body was also installed on the left side of the car body, as seen on the K5(E) at Batterie Todt. Two swiveling hooks for stowing the ladder flat against the side of the body are visible. *Pierre-Olivier Buan*

The lower section of the ladder is fully extended. Much like a modern-day extension ladder, the sections, when raised in their stowed positions, are held by swiveling hooks on the ladder; two of these hooks are visible at the top of the photograph. *Pierre-Olivier Buan*

The ammunition-handling platform on top of the generator housing of the K5(E) at Batterie Todt is viewed from the rear of the car body. The Ausf. D had two sets of trolley tracks on the platform, while the Ausf. C had one. *Pierre-Olivier Buan*

An ammunition trolley sits in its tracks atop the generator housing. The projectile was always placed at the center of the trolley, with the powder bags and the cartridge stacked around it, so the projectile could be rammed straight into the breech. *Pierre-Olivier Buan*

The trolley is viewed from the front. On the tray atop the trolley are four grab handles: two on the front and two on the back. As shown in wartime photos in this book, the crane would hoist a complete round of ammunition on a tray from a supply car up to the trolley. The wooden decking that was once present is now gone. *Pierre-Olivier Buan*

The wheels of the trolley appear to be simplified replacements. To the side is the fold-down extension of the platform, missing its original wooden decking. In the background is the ammunition crane, including manual hand cranks. *Pierre-Olivier Buan*

The left side of the ammunition trolley is displayed. Small rollers would be installed on the lugs on the bottom of the ammunition tray, so it could be shunted around before being hoisted up to the trolley on the generator-housing deck. *Pierre-Olivier Buan*

The trolley and ammunition tray are viewed from behind. Before the loaded tray was hoisted from the supply car to the trolley, curved hangers were fitted over the notched lugs at the corners of the tray. These formed a rigid connection between the tray and the hoist cable. *Pierre-Olivier Buan*

An overall view of the ammunition crane on the K5(E) at Batterie Todt also shows the D-shaped platform with grille flooring. *Pierre-Olivier Buan*

Seen up close here are the winch, platform with grille floor, and guardrail of the ammunition crane of the K5(E) rail gun at Batterie Todt. There is a data plate on the cover of the cable drum of the winch. A clear view is also provided of the hand cranks. *Pierre-Olivier Buan*

On the left side of the generator housing of the K5(E) at Batterie Todt, most of the exhaust is missing, including the perforated guard and muffler. Behind the front door (*to the left*) was an electrical control panel. A detachable platform, also missing, was provided for the electricians to stand on while operating the generator. *Pierre-Olivier Buan*

As viewed from the front left corner of the generator housing, the trolley tracks are laid out loosely on the deck. The front ends of the farthest pair of tracks are curved toward the center of the roof of the generator housing. This was so the tracks would merge with the single set of tracks on the deck of the K5(E) car body. See the drawing on the opposite page for the design of the trolley tracks on the K5(E) Ausf. D. *Pierre-Olivier Buan*

Ausf. C Loading Platform

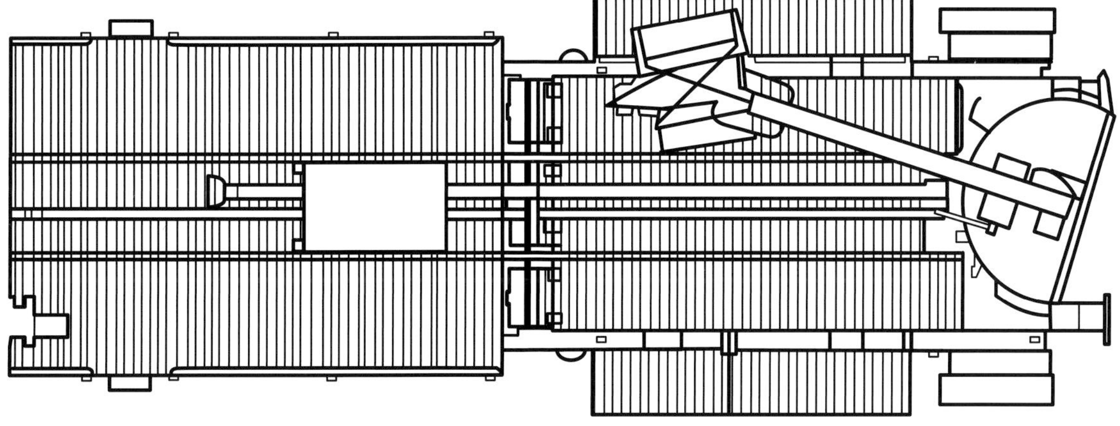

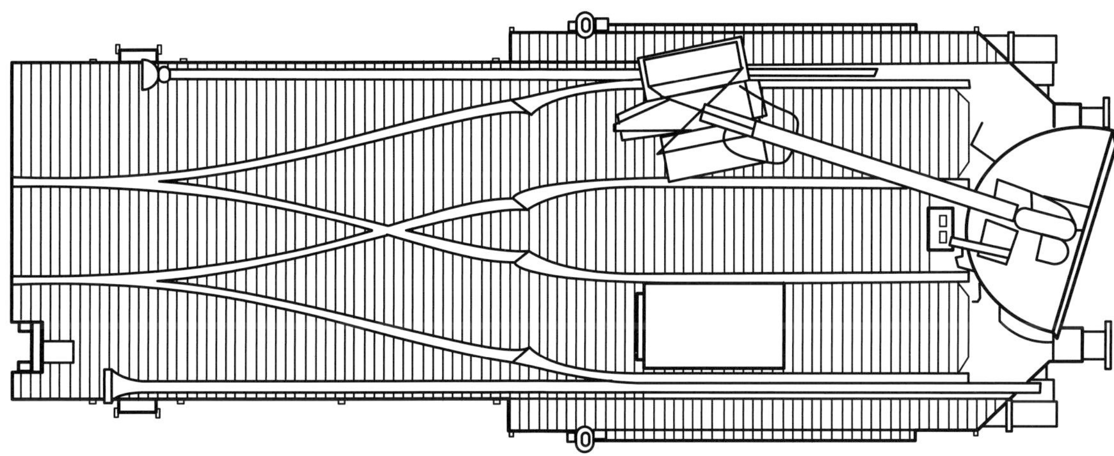

Ausf. D Loading Platform

In a view under the car body, the rear of the elevation equilibrator is at center. This device helped stabilize the elevation of the gun and reduced the force necessary to achieve elevation. At far left is a compressed air coupler with a shutoff valve, for connecting the air lines of the car body with those of the rear truck.

The elevation equilibrator of "Leopold" is viewed from slightly farther to the rear. At the center is the bottom of the gun cradle, with the rears of the elevation rods coupled to both of its sides. The force exerted by these rods on the bottom of the cradle exerted levering force on the cradle, and thus on the 28 cm gun, to effect elevation and depression.

In this view, the bottom of the 28 cm gun breech of the "Leopold" is at the top. Immediately below the breech is the recuperator, partially obscured by a crossbar that is coupled to the recuperator and the recoil buffers. Toward the bottom are the underside of the gun cradle, the rear ends of the elevation rods, and the rear of the elevation equilibrator.

The crossbar aft of the recoil buffers and recuperator is viewed close-up on the K5(E) at Batterie Todt. Details of the rear face of the recuperator, including the size and arrangement of the holes in it, are visible. To the bottom left is the rear of the left elevation rod, at its attachment point to the gun cradle. *Pierre-Olivier Buan*

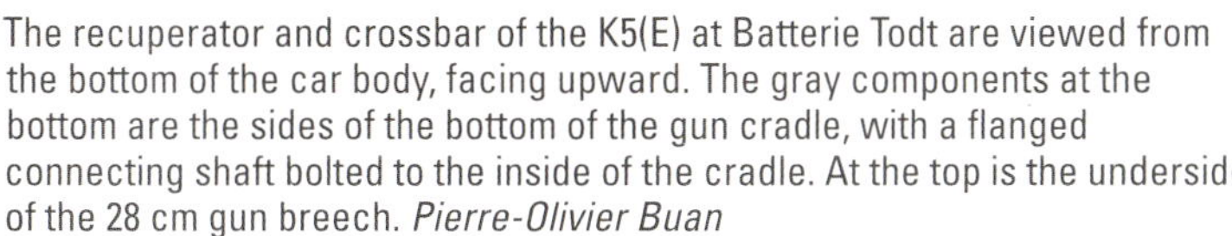

The recuperator and crossbar of the K5(E) at Batterie Todt are viewed from the bottom of the car body, facing upward. The gray components at the bottom are the sides of the bottom of the gun cradle, with a flanged connecting shaft bolted to the inside of the cradle. At the top is the underside of the 28 cm gun breech. *Pierre-Olivier Buan*

A hinged fixture with two lightening holes, the purpose of which is unclear, is mounted on each side of the bottom of the car body, more or less in line with the bottom of the gun cradle when the gun is in its lowered position for loading or travel. The elevation equilibrator in the background. The construction of the side of the car body, comprising several longitudinal walls with bracing, is apparent. *Pierre-Olivier Buan*

The counterpart of the hinged fixture seen on "Leopold" in the photo above is shown on the K5(E) at Batterie Todt, although this one is on the right side of the vehicle and is seen facing to the rear truck. A small chain holds the fixture in its stowed position.

The bottom of the gun cradle on the K5(E) at Batterie Todt is seen close-up from below the left side of the car body, facing forward. The heavy-duty, O-shaped connections at the rear ends of the elevation rods are painted gray and are connected to the sides of the cradle. The shank of the right elevation rod is visible above the equilibrator. *Pierre-Olivier Buan*

After arriving in Fort Lee, Virginia, "Leopold" is being reassembled. The 28 cm gun has been transported separately from the gondola and trucks (*left of center*) and is secured to a civilian lowboy semitrailer coupled to an Army-surplus M911 HET. With the 28 cm gun removed from the gondola, clear views of the lower part of its cradle and the left trunnion are visible. The large cylinder in the cradle, below the breech, is the recuperator. On the side of the cradle is the left recoil cylinder; another one is on the right side of the cradle. *Department of Defense*

Two mobile cranes have hoisted the 28 cm gun from the semitrailer. At this time, "Leopold" was painted in a fanciful two-color camouflage, with inexpertly executed lettering on the gondola. *Department of Defense*

The two cranes are maneuvering the 28 cm gun over the gondola at Fort Lee. The recuperator, visible in the cradle below the gun tube, acted to return the gun to firing position after being fired, while the recoil cylinders, on the sides of the cradle, buffered the recoil action of the gun upon being fired. *Department of Defense*

Crane riggers watch attentively as the 28 cm gun is lowered onto the trunnion bearings. The cover for the gunner's control panel, which originally was hinged at the top, had been immobilized by brackets, which were welded to the cover and the hull. Toward the right is the cartridge tray. *Department of Defense*

"Leopold" is seen from the front right after the 28 cm gun has been seated on the gondola. Rifling grooves are visible inside the muzzle. Brackets for mounting guardrails are still present along the top edges of the gondola. *Department of Defense*

With only two examples surviving in display settings, the K5(E) rail gun is among the rarest of heavy artillery weapons of World War II. Mounted on railroad cars, these guns allowed the Germans to take advantage of Europe's dense railway networks to rush hard-hitting artillery assets to hotspots as necessary. Although these guns sometimes wreaked havoc on Allied forces, particularly at the Anzio beachhead, they were a relic of an earlier time, and one that airpower had rendered obsolescent by World War II.

In early 2015, a project was initiated at Fort Lee to repaint "Leopold" in a more accurate scheme. Preparatory to painting, workers are getting ready to sandblast the entire artillery piece, to remove rust and paint scale. *Department of Defense*

The rear of the K5(E) has been sandblasted. Visible through the center access door on the rear of the gondola is the rear of the recuperator of the 28 cm gun. At the bottom are the rear buffers. *Department of Defense*

"Leopold" was repainted into the gray camouflage scheme it wore when new. Here the piece is viewed from the right side of the gun breech, looking forward. To the lower right is the right trunnion, to the front of which is the catwalk along the top of the gondola. *Department of Defense*

After "Leopold" was thoroughly sandblasted and prepped, the entire railroad gun was painted gray, which reportedly was the same shade it was painted during World War II. Parts of the previous camouflage paint are still visible on the forward parts of the gun tube and the front truck, including the wheels and springs. *Department of Defense*

The repainting of "Leopold" in 2015 also entailed the restoration of the wartime markings, as seen in this view from the left side of the gondola, facing to the rear. Among other markings is the Deutsche Reichsbahn Berlin number, 919219, on the truck as well as the center of the gondola. At the center are hand levers for the gun-elevation brakes. *Department of Defense*

"Leopold," as restored with gray camouflage and replica markings, is observed from the left rear. Visible between the forward part of the gun breech and the gun cradle are small steel strips, which were welded in place to immobilize the gun after it was tested at Aberdeen Proving Ground. *Department of Defense*

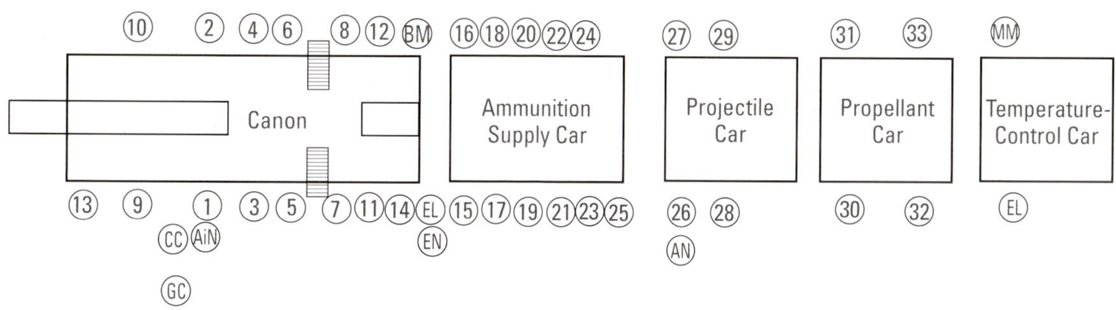

GC = gun commander
EN = noncommissioned officer, electrical
CC = car commander
MM = motor mechanic
AiN = noncommissioned officer, gun aimer
AN = noncommissioned officer, ammunition
BM = battery mechanic
EL = electrician

Numbered positions were occupied by enlisted men.

Crew positions

After the 2015 restoration of its camouflage paint, "Leopold" was placed in long-term storage in a building at the US Army Ordnance Training Support Facility, Fort Lee, Virginia. The building, which also houses one of the US M65 atomic cannons, is not open to the public. *Author*